I0410990

Executive Summary

Title: Cross-Domain Synergy: Warfare in the 21st Century

Author: Major John B. Gallemore, United States Air Force

Thesis: Due to budget constraints, high operations tempo, poor training structure, and current operational planning paradigms the United States Military is not postured to conduct effective and efficient Cross Domain Synergy (XDS) in full-spectrum combat operations against a near-peer adversary.

Discussion: Today's strategic environment is dynamic and rapidly changing. Warfighting domains, including air, land, and sea, where the United States has dominated for almost one half-century, are increasingly being tested by traditional states, as well as non-state actors. Space, although an extremely critical domain, is only affected by a finite few in the world due to the amount of capital required to conduct operations in this regime. In contrast, very little capital or infrastructure is required to operate in the Cyber domain making it easy to contest. Globalization has facilitated the ability of less capable nations to garner critical warfighting technology. The parity in technology between nations at war is no longer as great. This leveled the playing field and allowed for non-state actors to have dramatic influence on powerful nations, which has not been the case in the past. Historically, only nations with large financial reserves and mass expenditures on military capabilities waged global warfare. Globalization fundamentally opens the door for almost any nation or non-state actor with an agenda to wage warfare in the cyber domain. Now more than ever before in United States history, it is imperative the United States Military develop and maintain the ability to effectively and efficiently execute XDS in full-spectrum combat operations.

Conclusion: Fiscal limitations, unsustainable operations tempos, inadequate training, and current operational planning paradigms and processes have put the United States Military in a perilous situation and hindered its ability to conduct effective and efficient defense. The greatest calamity that could arise from these realities is the inability to address XDS in full-spectrum combat operations against a near-peer adversary.

Illustrations

Table of Contents

Preface

I have spent 14 years as an instructor pilot and flight evaluator in the United States Air Force. Prior to attending Marine Corps Command and Staff College, I had the opportunity to fulfill duties as Project Officer for Exercise RED FLAG at Nellis AFB, NV. What I witnessed during the execution of this exercise inspired me to write my masters thesis on the United States Military's inability to currently conduct cross-domain synergy against a near-peer adversary.

Effective and efficient cross-domain synergy is imperative to success in 21st century warfare. This report compares national strategic level documents mandating cross-domain synergy and points out the United States Military shortcomings in fulfilling these mandates. I conducted research using sources across the various United States Armed Services and culminated my research with the sole exercise currently conducted in the Department of Defense to practice and conduct cross-domain synergy against a near-peer adversary, Exercise RED FLAG.

I would like to acknowledge Dr. Matthew Flynn, Marine Corps University, for his guidance in the construction of this masters thesis. Furthermore, I would like to acknowledge Major Raymond Daniel, United States Air Force Joint Tactics Squadron Director of Operations, and Major Aaron Jelinek, United States Air Force Defense Fellow, for their insight and direction.

September 11, 2001 gave the United States a new focus and perspective on the nation's well-being, global influence, and deterrence strategies. Subsequently, the current National Security Strategy (NSS), as well as the National Military Strategy (NMS), has taken astronomical steps forward in pursuing the security of the nation at home and abroad. However, more than a decade at war has hampered the United States and the United States Military's ability to focus on certain requirements of the NSS. Due to budget constraints, high operations tempo, poor training structure, and current operational planning paradigms the United States Military is not postured to conduct effective and efficient Cross Domain Synergy (XDS) in full-spectrum combat operations against a near-peer adversary.

Today's strategic environment is dynamic and rapidly changing. Warfighting domains, including air, land, and sea, where the United States has dominated for almost one half-century, are increasingly being tested by traditional states, as well as non-state actors. Space, although an extremely critical domain, is only affected by a finite few in the world due to the amount of capital required to conduct operations in this regime. Cyber, on-the-other hand, is a domain in which it is extremely easy to contest and requires little infrastructure or capital to conduct operations. Globalization has facilitated the ability of less capable nations to garner critical warfighting technology. The technology parity between nations at war is no longer as great. This leveled the playing field and allowed for non-state actors to have dramatic influence on powerful nations, which has not been the case in the past. Historically, only nations with large financial reserves and mass expenditures on military capabilities waged global warfare. The 2011 NMS highlights the fact that through globalization:

> States are developing anti -access and area-denial (A2AD) capabilities and strategies to constrain U nited States and international freedom of action. These states are rapidly acquiring technologies, such as missiles and autonomously-piloted platforms that challenge our ability to project power from the global commons and increase our operational risk. Meanwhile, enabling and war-fighting domains of space and cyberspace are simultaneously more

critical for our operations, yet more vulnerable to malicious actions. The space environment is becoming more congested, contested, and competitive. Some states are conducting or condoning cyber intrusions that foreshadow the growing threat in this globally connected domain. The cyber threat is expanded and exacerbated by lack of international norms, difficulties of attribution, low barriers to entry, and the relative ease of developing potent capabilities.[1]

Fundamentally, globalization opens the door for almost any nation or non-state actor with an agenda to wage warfare in the cyber domain. Now more than ever before in the history of the United States, it is imperative the United States Military develop and maintain the ability to effectively and efficiently execute XDS in full-spectrum combat operations.

XDS DEFINED

Effective and efficient XDS blends all domains into a coordinated warfighting kinetic and non-kinetic effort to defeat an enemy in any situation. Effective XDS allows seamless combat operations and force projection. It requires each service to act interdependently, effectively, and efficiently by merging core warfighting functions to defeat an adversary in any battlespace domain. In January 2012, General Martin Dempsey, Chairman of the Joint Chiefs of Staff, endorsed this end by stating in the Joint Operating Access Concept (JOAC):

> To meet that challenge, future joint forces will leverage cross-domain synergy—the complementary vice merely additive employment of capabilities in different domains such that each enhances the effectiveness and compensates for the vulnerabilities of the others—to establish superiority in some combination of domains that will provide the freedom of action required by the mission. The combination of domain superiorities will vary with the situation, depending on the enemy's capabilities and the requirements of the mission. Superiority in any domain may not be widespread or permanent; it more often will be local and temporary. Attaining cross-domain synergy to overcome future access challenges will require a greater degree of integration than ever before. Additionally this integration will have to occur at lower echelons, generating the tempo that is often critical to exploiting fleeting local opportunities for disrupting the enemy system, and will require the full inclusion of space and cyberspace operations into the traditional air-land-sea battlespace.[2]

As much credence that has been given to this view in strategic level documents such as the NSS, NMS, DSG and the JOAC, little to no literature outside of these strategic level theories has addressed this concept leaving it greatly underdeveloped. In order to fully understand XDS, it must be put in context against a near-peer adversary. This thesis looks to establish XDS as fundamental to our interwar thinking and how the shaping of 21st century budget constructs, training paradigms, Joint force structuring, and Joint force training should be conducted.

Globalization and the dynamic nature of the strategic environment make it essential for the United States Military to be able to conduct effective and efficient XDS in full-spectrum combat operations against a near-peer adversary. Warfighting domains according to the 2012 Defense Strategic Guidance (DSG) are air, land, maritime, space, and cyberspace.[3] The interlinked domains of air, space, and cyberspace allow for a rapid and mass exchange of knowledge, information, commodities, people, and commerce that are critical to the global economic system. Collectively, these domains are crucial and symbiotic channels for America's projection and sustainment of its power. Cross Domain Synergy, or XDS, is the ability of a nation to amalgamate the different warfighting domains into a concerted effort to deter and defeat aggression.

BUDGET IMPACTS

A recent budget reduction implication study conducted by the Brookings Institute stated, "the major disadvantage of the recently announced (military personnel and equipment) withdrawals is that they will reduce opportunities for the United States and European ground units to exercise together, with potential implications for interoperability."[4] As the characteristics of war shift into a more hybrid state, joint/multi-national interoperability and consequently the ability to merge domains will be instrumental in bringing the full capabilities of the United States and its allies' militaries to bear on an adversary. Similarly, a memorandum published on January 7, 2013 by Secretary of the Air Force Michael Donley and Chief of Staff of the Air Force, Gen Mark Welsh stated the following regarding potential results of budget reductions:

> The defense strategy requires the Air Force to maintain a high state of readiness across the total force. We cannot execute the strategy from a tiered readiness posture. The flying hour reductions will compel us to focus almost exclusively on current missions such as training pipelines,

Operation ENDURING FREEDOM spin-up and other deployments while sacrificing preparedness for contingencies and Operations Plans (OPLANS). Thus the 18% cut will be disproportionately applied across the force; deployed and next-to-deploy units will be minimally cut, leaving remaining units to take the brunt of the cuts and stand down for extended periods. These units will likely fall to the lowest readiness levels and will require extensive time and funding to recover.[5]

This is just one of the United States Military service chiefs addressing the results drastic cuts will have on readiness and operational capability. However, all services will experience a similar decline in readiness due to an inability to train and operate in full-spectrum combat operations requiring XDS to defeat an enemy. As a result, these budget cuts will directly impact the United States ability to fulfill national strategic and security objectives.

Throughout history, it has been imperative that nations maintain the ability to effectively and efficiently conduct XDS in order to fulfill national security requirements. Prior to the 1950s, these domains were limited to air, land, and maritime. Once the United States and the rest of the world entered the space-centric center of activity, new warfighting domains were added with the evolution of space-based capabilities and with the addition of cyberspace. With new domains comes the challenge of developing and revising new tactics, techniques, and procedures (TTPs) in order to synchronize battlespace efforts across all domains in an effective and efficient manner and thereby winning America's wars.

The last time the United States conducted a war in a multi-domain environment against a "relatively" near-peer adversary were Operations DESERT SHIELD and DESERT STORM. Although combat operations were conducted in the air, land, maritime, and space domains, during these campaigns very few operations were conducted in the cyber realm. As a result, the United States has not had the opportunity to fully test its ability to conduct XDS in full-spectrum combat operations against a near-peer adversary.

In January 2012, the Department of Defense (DOD) released its annual *Defense Budget Priorities and Choices* report outlining its fiscal plan for the next ten years. The single most alarming fact highlighted in this report was the reduction in defense department spending. It reads: "the department's investment choices for FY2013 to 2017 were derived from this guidance and conform to the 2011 Budget Control Act reducing Defense Department future expenditures by approximately $487 billion over the next decade or $259 billion over the next five years."[6] One of the main tenants contained in the 2012 NSS states:

> We will continue to rebalance our military capabilities to excel at counterterrorism, counterinsurgency, stability operations, and meeting increasingly sophisticated security threats, while ensuring our force is ready to address the full range of military operations. This includes preparing for increasingly sophisticated adversaries, deterring and defeating aggression in anti-access environments, and defending the United States and supporting civil authorities at home.[7]

Given the reductions in spending, there is not enough money to meet DOD needs. For example, the NSS, as well as the NMS, made cyberspace a defensive priority. Accordingly, funds have been allocated in support of this guidance. However, the multi-billion dollar cuts in the current defense budget require reductions in programs such as the Joint Strike Fighter, and the elimination of six United States Air Force (USAF) tactical fighter squadrons, one USAF training squadron, the new Expeditionary Fighter Vehicle (EFV), and latest Amphibious Assault Ship.[8] The United States Military must now attempt to equip and train the warfighting force to fight America's wars in support of the NSS with an aging fleet of equipment.

Similar to the NSS, the NMS highlights how critical the ability to conduct operations across all warfighting domains is to the nation's ability to project power. The 2011 NMS specifically lists priorities to shape military strategy:

> Joint assured access to the global commons and cyberspace constitutes a core aspect of U.S. national security and remains an enduring mission for the Joint Force. The global commons and globally connected domains constitute the connective tissue upon which all nations' security and prosperity depend. The maritime domain enables the bulk of the joint force's forward deployment and sustainment, as well as the commerce that underpins the global economic system.[9]

Even though national strategic guidance requires the United States Military to possess XDS capable forces ready to conduct operations across the entire spectrum of battle, balanced force apportionment is becoming far more difficult for Combatant Commanders, as well as DOD strategists and planners. Inadequate training opportunities and lack of commander and operator knowledge are just several of the issues commanders face when fielding forces in support of combat operations or operational planning.

OPERATIONS TEMPO IMPACTS

The final withdrawal of United States troops from Operation IRAQI FREEDOM occurred on December 16, 2011, concluding over nine continuous years of war.[10] Furthermore, Operation ENDURING FREEDOM has entered its eleventh year of sustained combat operations. The toll these concurrent operations in Iraq and Afghanistan have taken on not only the troops, but also the warfighting material will probably never be quantified. The sheer mental degradation in combat forces is staggering. The marked increase in cases of Post-Traumatic Stress Disorder (PTSD), tens of thousands of permanently disabled combat veterans, and broken families will never be fully appreciated. A report published by the United States Army Sergeant Majors Academy highlights:

> While evaluating the impact of long deployments on military readiness we discovered that military readiness is diminished. The impact of the military family structure has been immense. The military family contributes greatly to military readiness. The service member must have a stable family to properly focus on the combat mission at hand. We discovered that the effects of long frequent deployments have contributed to the breakdown of the military family. Divorce rates and domestic violence have increased during the Global War on Terror. This is directly responsible as soldiers are under remarkable stress due to the frequent deployments and their continuous departure from their family.[11]

The current operations tempo alone has decreased the United States Military's capability to effectively conduct operations. The NMS highlights the point that traumatic brain injury and post traumatic stress have become similarly devastating, affecting hundreds of thousands of service members and veterans and "in many ways, these issues are the greatest threat to our people and present a strategic risk to our institution."[12] Coupled with inadequate training and budget constraints, the military is currently not capable of fulfilling its mission as outlined in the NMS.

The amount of time away from primary duty stations has dramatically increased with sustained military operations and force restructuring. Service members are often away from their homes to attend professional military educational development, train for war, conduct humanitarian aid, carry out peacekeeping missions, and take part in combat operations.[13] Some service members have experienced their second, third and fourth tour in Iraq and/or Afghanistan, and it is not uncommon for troops to be home for six months before they deploy again.[14] Currently members of the armed forces can be deployed continuously in support of contingency operations between four to twelve months depending on the branch of service and incessantly experience dwell cycles of 1:1 or less.

For example, in a report provided to the President and Congress, the United States Army recounted of the approximately 640,000 soldiers serving on active duty, 315,000 are deployed or forward stationed in more than 120 countries to support operations in Iraq, Afghanistan and other theaters around the globe.[15] More recent information reported in the Quadrennial Defense Review Report stated that on any given day nearly 350,000 members of the Armed Forces are deployed in approximately 130 countries.[16] The 2008 Status of Forces Survey of Active Duty Members reported on average military members spend 77 nights away from home in a single year.[17] An additional indicator of an unsustainable operations tempo is the fact that over 75% of surveyed active duty members feel that they are "neither well prepared or poorly prepared" to perform the wartime duties.[18] Finally, as of September 11, 2001 the average United States Military active duty member has deployed 2.4 times for an average of nine months at time.[19] With the increase in deployments and work hours, in excess of 50 to 55 hours a week, it is important to determine if the strain placed on the combat forces has negatively effected the ability of the United States Military to fulfill the NSS and NMS requirements.[20]

In addition to the strain placed on military service members, the United States Military's warfighting equipment is on the brink of unserviceability. The added demands of protracted warfare have brought unprogrammed fatigue on an already aging fleet of equipment. As one study highlights, "the impact on equipment is highly recognizable through the struggle to properly equip military forces, through combat stressed equipment, and through the costly repair and replacement of equipment, which has caused a decline in readiness."[21] The 2011 NMS states:

> We must carefully manage the impact of the wars on our military – especially our people – and shape our military for the future. Defense budget projections indicate that leaders must continue to plan for and make difficult choices between current and future challenges. We underestimate at our peril the stresses of sustained combat operations on our equipment and people.[22]

With military deployments reaching unprecedented levels, the United States Military's hardware is aging at a rate in which replacement assets cannot fulfill requirements.[23] In fact, a study performed by the Office of the Secretary of Defense (OSD) reported, "in current combat operations, equipment usage rates have run two to eight times higher than comparable peacetime rates."[24] An M1 Abrams tank incurs approximately 800 miles of annual use during peacetime operations.[25] However, since the beginning of the Global War on Terror (GWOT), the M1 Abrams is averaging 3500 miles annually.[26] The M1 is not the only military asset facing this crisis. The Bradley tanks historically have incurred 850 miles annually but increase to 3600 miles annually during combat operations.[27] Similarly, High Mobility Multipurpose Wheeled Vehicle (HMMWV) use has increased from 2600 miles in peacetime to 7300 miles annually.[28] The increased demands on warfighting equipment and focus towards general purpose forces conducting counterinsurgency (COIN) and stability operations has limited the United States

Military's ability to focus on the needs of future conflicts.

Compiling this myriad of issues is a recipe for a national security disaster. All of these pressures and challenges are a direct result of an unsustainable operations tempo thereby directly affecting the nations ability to not only wage war, but more importantly, conduct warfare in a cross-domain synergistic environment when pitted against a near-peer adversary. The United States Military's current combat forces are extremely well postured to conduct COIN and stability operations in terms of warfighter knowledge, expertise, and COIN equipment. However, deployment rates, operations tempo, and exhausted warfighting materiel are such that the number one combat asset of the country, the warfighter, is limited in his/her ability to conduct XDS.

The current NSS requires the DOD to fulfill "United States defense commitments with tailored approaches to deterrence and ensuring the United States Military continues to have the necessary capabilities across all domains—land, air, sea, space, and cyber."[29] Requiring the United States Military to conduct on-going operations in Afghanistan, while apportioning forces to conduct full-spectrum combat functions under the current operations tempo, is not feasible. The vast majority of warfighters in the United States Military have been operating in a "stove-pipe" environment. They are extremely capable of bringing their combat power to bear with regards to their niche expertise. However, when asked to conduct XDS in support of full-spectrum combat operations, their lack of integration, training, and operational experience shows dramatically. This is not due to lack of weapons system knowledge or expertise but the nation's operational focus on supporting COIN and stability operations.

TRAINING STRUCTURE IMPACTS

Similar to the effects the current lack of integration and operational experience are having on combat forces, the current training structure in the United States Military is inadequate to employ XDS effectively to conduct full-spectrum combat operations against a near-peer adversary. The purpose of the NMS is to provide the ways and means on how the military fulfills requirements outlined by the NSS. The 2011 NMS clearly states, "we will conduct more full-spectrum joint, combined, interagency, and multinational training, exercises and experimentation."[30] However, budget constraints resulted in the United States Air Force Air Combat Command (ACC) reducing the number of training opportunities from five per year to three per year in FY12 and canceled all remaining exercises for FY13 and FY14.[31] Only one of these exercises utilizes XDS to conduct full-spectrum combat operations in a joint, multi-national environment with the nation's closest allies. The other two exercises each year are a mixture of joint and/or multi-national, but are not conducted at a level representative of a near-peer adversary. This is only one example of how the United States Military, as well as the United States Air Force, is unable to meet training requirements in support of the current NMS or NSS mandates related to XDS. More budget cuts threaten to curtail even this training.

Due to limited training operations, many Combat Air Force (CAF) squadrons are only meeting the minimum requirements set forth in Air Force Instruction (AFI) training regulations and guidelines to maintain combat mission ready status. For example, aircrews are required to fly eight sorties per month as an experienced aviator and nine as an inexperienced aviator.[32] These numbers have been reduced due to budget constraints over the past two years, as previous sorties requirements were nine for an experienced aviator and 10 for an inexperienced aviator.[33] However, an F-16 service life enhancement program (SLEP) study indicated, "flying 13 sorties per month would do away with the need for a squadron pre-combat spin-up program."[34] Flying additional training sorties would eliminate the need for a pre-combat spin-up allowing at a minimum, four to five additional training sorties per month to focus on missions outside of those required to conduct operations in contingency situations. Additional training missions would allow fighter squadrons to maintain combat mission ready status for all pilots, not just a select few, and enhance overall force lethality.[35] The same conclusions derived from the study on F-16s and the Air Force can be applied to Marine Corps and Navy fighter aircraft squadrons. The NSS warns, "when we overuse our military might, or fail to invest in or deploy complementary tools, or act without partners, then our military is overstretched."[36] Unfortunately, today's current operations tempo is not affording the United States Military's maritime, land, air, space, and cyberspace practitioners this opportunity.

Two examples of the United States Military's inability to conduct joint/multi-national XDS in full-spectrum combat operations against a near-peer adversary occurred during Exercise RED FLAG 12-3 and Exercise RED FLAG 13-3. The Air Force executed RED FLAG 12-3 from 20 Feb – 16 Mar 2012 and RED FLAG 13-3 from 21 Feb – 15 Mar 2013.[37] Participants from across the Department of Defense and several of the United States closest allies, including the United Kingdom and Australia, organized as an Air and Space Expeditionary Wing (AEW), practiced integration, planning, and execution of joint and combined composite multi-national force operations in a realistic simulated full-spectrum combat environment. All units participated in day and night missions during this 3-week exercise conducted on the Nevada Test and Training Range (NTTR). Participants included units from the Joint Information Operations Warfare Center (JIOWC), Joint Electronic Protection for Air Combat (JEPAC), Joint Air Operations Center (JAOC), United States Air Warfare Center (USAWC), United States Air Force Weapons School (USAFWS), United States Air Force (USAF), United States Army (USA), United States Marine Corps (USMC), United States Navy (USN), British Royal Air

Force (RAF), Royal Australian Air Force (RAAF), Defense Advanced Research Projects Agency (DARPA), United States Air Force Reserve (USAFR), Air National Guard (ANG), and United States Special Operations Command (USSOCOM) participated in Exercises RED FLAG 12-3 and RED FLAG 13-3.[38] Participants operated under the Joint Forces Air Component Commander (JFACC) in accordance with Joint Publication 3-30.[39] The RED FLAG 12-3 and RED FLAG 13-3 JFACC developed a joint air operations plan (JAOP), Air Operations Directive (AOD), and an Air Tasking Order (ATO) to facilitate mission execution. Mission planners utilized elements of the Joint Operational Planning Process (JOPP) to develop each missions course of action (COA) and built targeting matrices in accordance with JP 3-60 Joint Targeting Process.[40]

Participating units fought as a cohesive coalition that integrated operational level force enablers and operators of non-kinetic effects (NKE) weapons systems with kinetic flying units. Each flying unit in the Large Force Exercise (LFE) was tasked to fly Offensive Counter-Air (OCA), Defensive Counter-Air (DCA), Close Air Support (CAS), Air Interdiction (AI), Killer-Scout, Suppression of Enemy Air Defense (SEAD), Destruction of Enemy Air Defense (DEAD), Intelligence/Surveillance/Reconnaissance (ISR), Command and Control (C2) sorties, with some strikers responding to dynamic targeting (DT) taskings. During the LFE, combat search and rescue (CSAR) procedures were practiced utilizing ground based CSAR parties in order to exfiltrate downed aircrew. C2, ISR, cyber, space, and network warfare participants integrated their operations with efforts of all other units to train in a cross-domain synergistic environment against a near-peer adversary.[41]

This multi-national, joint exercise provided a realistic simulated anti-access, area denial (A2AD) environment for aircrews, operational level force enablers, and operators of non-flying weapons systems from the USAF, USMC, USN, USA, RAF, and RAAF to hone their combat skills. Simultaneous simulated combat operations were conducted in which blue forces flew large force exercise (LFE) missions in the northern bombing ranges. Non-kinetic operations were conducted on the Joint Information Operations Range (JIOR) and the 24th Space Range.[42] The Blue Force was opposed by air, cyber, space, information, and ground threat simulators (Red Forces) operating in a realistic, simulated integrated air defense system (sIADS).[43]

The strategic objective of Exercise RED FLAG is designed for less experienced combat operators across all warfighting domains, while using higher-level operational and strategic concepts. The exercise also gives more experienced operators and non-kinetic effects (NKE) members the opportunity to learn and experience the roles of Mission and Package Commanders, as well as facilitate exposure to full-spectrum XDS. A direct observation included in the Exercise RED FLAG 12-3 After Action Report (AAR) states:

> Operators at the tactical level were not proficient or trained to effectively execute cross-domain Synergy (XDS). Currently, there is only one DoD venue to train and operate in a full-spectrum simulated combat operation. As a result, there is a severe lack of understanding of different domain capabilities. Operators are very good in their MDS but use "stove-piped" and antiquated methods in their mission planning processes.[44]

Exercise RED FLAG 13-3 was conducted almost one year to date after RED FLAG 12-3 and the results were the same. Colonel Tod Fingal, Commander 414 Combat Training Squadron (CTS) and Exercise RED FLAG, noted "our forces lack the ability to 'force package.' Force packaging skills have atrophied over the past 10 years and our ability to pull together the right force in a dynamic, A2AD environment has waned."[45] Col Fingal elaborated by adding:

> Our current C2 (CAOC/AWACS/etc) construct for the COIN fight in Iraq and Afghanistan has created an environment of centralized control and centralized execution. To dominate the battlespace against a near-peer adversary, we need to train our forces to operate in a centralized control and decentralized execution environment. In an A2AD environment, we cannot afford to get permission from the CAOC for everything. It works in COIN, but not against a near-peer.[46]

The results of Exercises RED FLAG 12-3 and RED FLAG 13-3 are indicative of a combat force that has been subjected to an unsustainable operations tempo hampering training to effectively fulfill the NSS, NMS, and DSG. Furthermore, fiscal restraints have limited the warfighters ability to fully bring the United States Military's combat power to bear. All of this is in direct conflict with the current Capstone Concepts for Joint Operations (CCJO) 2012 that states, "while the United States Military maintains unique advantages in every domain, it is our ability to project force across domains that so often generates our decisive advantage."[47]

PLANNING PARADIGM IMPACTS

In addition to deficiencies in operational and tactical level execution and poor training concepts, "mission planners were very inefficient with their use of available planning time. Their lack of proficiency in integration of air, space, and cyber effects caused many planners to not have time to thoroughly develop contingency plans and well thought out contracts between key players."[48] Although processes such as the Joint Operations Planning Process (JOPP), Military Decision Making Process (MDMP), and the Marine Corps Planning Process (MCPP) exist, current commanders, operators, and mission planners are not proficient at employing these constructs in a cross-domain synergistic environment.

Several of the deficiencies in mission planning would be solved with increased opportunities for the warfighter to participate in full-spectrum combat training exercises utilizing XDS such as RED FLAG. The CCJO specifically states, "forces must train and exercise standardized tactics, techniques, and procedures in both Joint and Service-specific training."[49] Affording this opportunity to our young warfighters, as well as senior leaders, to participate in multi-national, Joint force training would enhance the breadth of knowledge across all domains.

Many of the issues mission planners and mission executors faced resulted from lack of complimentary weapons systems capability knowledge. Without knowing the specific capabilities that each weapon system, both kinetic and non-kinetic, bring to bear results in cross-domain synchronization, an inadequate and improper response to adversary hostilities as opposed to cross-domain synergy. The CJCS feels Joint training is so critical to the development of warfighters they have developed a strategy called the Joint Learning Continuum (JLC). The JLC provides a systematic approach to the professional development throughout a warfighters career.

Figure 1.1 is a graphic depiction published in the Chairman of the Joint Chiefs of Staff Instruction (CJCSI), 15 Mar 2012 outlining the chairman's vision.[50]

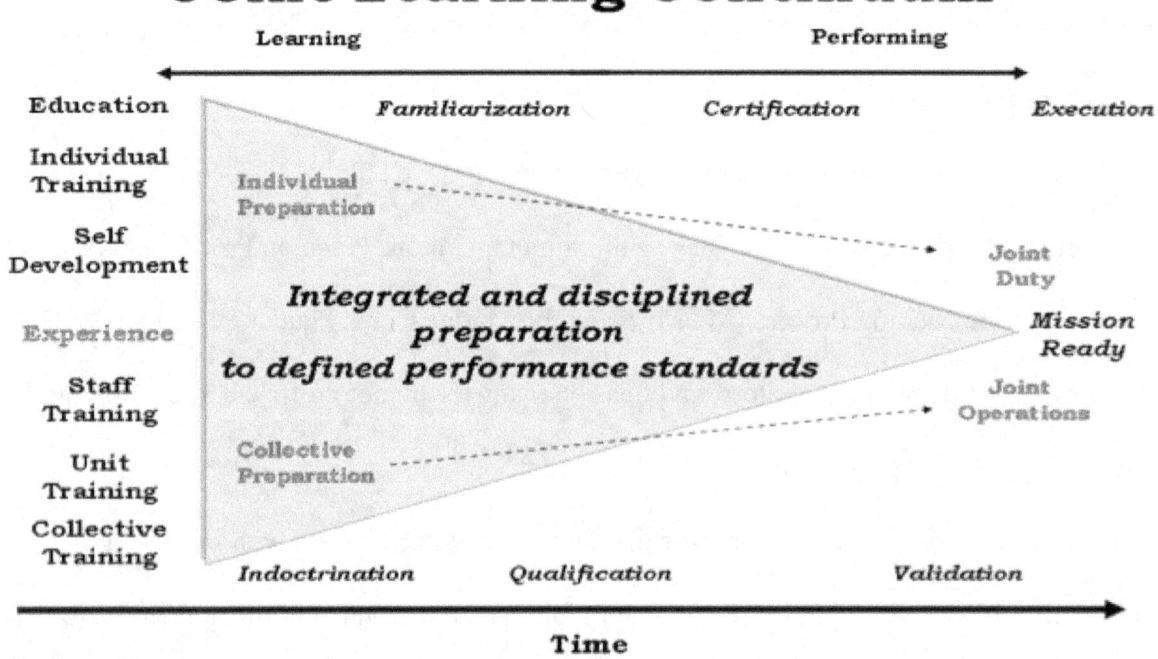

The CJCSI, 15 Mar 2012, defines joint training as:

> …instruction and applied exercises for acquiring and retaining knowledge, skills, abilities, and attitudes (KSAAs) necessary to complete specific tasks. As defined in DoDD 1322.18, joint training is training, including mission rehearsals of individuals, units, and staffs using joint doctrine and tactics, techniques, and procedures (TTPs) to prepare joint forces or joint staffs to respond to strategic, operational, or tactical requirements considered necessary by the CCDRs to execute assigned or anticipated missions.[51]

Training and education are not mutually exclusive. Elements of education and training are most often blended in application to achieve desired learning objectives and ultimate performance outcomes. However, as crucial as operator development is to senior leadership, current budget constraints and operational tempo do not allow the warfighter to get the training required to effectively and efficiently execute XDS.

In addition to the JLC, the CJCS has issued publications addressing Joint operations, Joint planning, and Joint leadership constructs. The CJCS Pub 3-0, as well as The Planner's Handbook for Operational Design are two such publications. The 3-0 defines one of the Common Operating Precepts as the ability to "achieve and maintain unity of effort within the Joint force and between the joint force and interorganizational partners."[52] An essential skill of any Joint Forces Commander (JFC) and/or planner is to match the mission of each Service to its core capabilities. Furthermore, each Service component's mission should create an amalgamation, or XDS, with that of its sister services. This in essence allows the actions of each component to enrich the competencies and bound the weaknesses of the others. In order to accomplish this "complementary synergy, a complete and holistic understanding of the particular capabilities and limitations that each component brings to the operation is imperative."[53] The JFC must be able to visualize operations and distinguish the "preconditions that enable each component to optimize its own contribution and then determine how the other components might help to produce them."[54] Current commanders and operating forces across the United States Military do not possess the ability to accomplish "complementary synergy" or XDS due to their fundamental lack of knowledge across the different operating domains.

The problem of Joint synergy is not new, but arguably far more dynamic in today's battlespace and drastically different in cross-domain synergistic environments. Carl von Clausewitz states in his book *On War,* "the commander's talents are given greatest scope in rough hilly country. Mountains allow him too little real command over his scattered units and he is unable to control them all; in open country, control is a simple matter and does not test his ability to the fullest."[55] Never has this been more evident than in today's operating environment. Commanders, planners, and operators alike are asked to conduct Joint operations integrating effects across all domains of the battlespace seamlessly, applying combat power across the domains with enhanced integration and effects. However, the domains are so diverse and require such an enormous understanding to grasp, even a single domain, that mere academic training is not sufficient to afford a commander, planner, or operator the understanding required to effectively conduct XDS. The solution to enhancing the United States Military's understanding of executing XDS in Joint operations is increased frequency in conducting Joint operations training in a full-spectrum, multi-domain environments.

One can consider operational art as an attempt to facilitate effective XDS in a Joint environment. *The Planner's Handbook for Operational Design* states the following:

> Operational design's initial focus is on helping the JFC visualize the operational environment, understand the problem that must be solved, and develop a broad operational approach that can create the desired end state.[56]

However, the fundamental flaw in this concept lies in the basic assumption that a commander, at a minimum, must have some understanding of the capabilities that his forces bring to the battlespace. The diverse nature of core competencies in the United States Military today do not allow a commander the ability to fully grasp their operational capabilities without first-hand experience in either combat or a training environment utilizing effective and efficient XDS in full-spectrum combat operations.

Emerging domains such as cyberspace are so singularly diverse and vaguely understood it is impossible to expect a JFC or even a staff planner to fully understand how to integrate their capabilities into mission planning unless the individual has first-hand operational and tactical-level knowledge. Domains as complex and vast as space and cyber are never fully understood or appreciated through a mere academic understanding. To effectively and efficiently integrate domains such as cyber and space into the other battlespace domains, a basic operational level of understanding must exist. Commanders, planners, and operators cannot rely on academic application alone and expect effective or accurate results. JP 3-0 states the following regarding operational design and understanding:

> The operational level links the tactical employment of forces to national and military strategic objectives. The focus at this level is on the design, planning, and execution of operations using operational art: the application of creative imagination by commanders and staffs—supported by their skill, knowledge, and experience—to design strategies, campaigns, and major operations and organize and employ military forces. JFCs and component commanders use operational art to determine how, when, where, and for what purpose major forces will be employed and to influence the adversary's disposition before combat.[57]

The attempt to mitigate this gap in commander knowledge is through the use of their staff and/or subject matter experts utilizing constructs derived from the JOPP to develop a commander's course of action. Inappropriately, the basic assumption that is made regarding a commander's knowledge is applied to the mission planners. As a result, a fundamental lack of understanding and knowledge from the operator level to the command level exists in the United States Military forces and severely stifles its ability to conduct effect and efficient XDS in full-spectrum combat operations.

Joint Forces Commanders and operational planners can use established processes such as the JLC to enhance their subject matter expertise. Nevertheless, an effective planning process to put their expertise into practice does not exist to fully legitimize their increased knowledge. Processes such as the JOPP, MDMP, and MCPP are an excellent framework with which to guide commanders, operations, and planners. Conversely, as mentioned earlier, these processes rely on specific assumptions or intangible skill sets commanders and planners possess. Although the JOPP, MDMP, and MCPP have utility, they possess several key flaws that make the process ineffective in implementing a cohesive plan for planning and conducting cross-domain synergistic type operations.

The first flaw in the current construct of military planning processes is a lack of modernization. Both MCPP and MDMP do not accurately portray the effects that operational planners and commanders need to be successful. Although terms such as, end-ways-means and essential-implied-specified tasks, are used to propagate thought regarding effects, planners can easily get lost in semantics between the terms. A simple concept, such as effects-based warfare allows commanders and planners to focus on the true end-state or desired effects for the operation. Maj Raymond Daniel, senior instructor pilot at the USAFWS and Director of Operations for the 561st Joint Tactics Squadron wrote:

> Since the military transitioned to an effects-based style of warfare during Desert Storm, planners must now consider how to best achieve the desired strategic outcome or effect on the enemy through synergistic and cumulative application of the full range of military and non-military capabilities (to include kinetic and non-kinetic effects). The various levels of the effects (first, second, and third order) must also be considered and addressed. Focusing on effects, rather than attrition, enables a highly coordinated level of inter- service, interagency, and international cooperation.[58]

Utilizing effects-based planning would facilitate a more synergistic, effective, and efficient planning process in a cross-domain environment and enhance inter-service and interagency operability.

Another flaw in the current military planning processes are the lack of executable facets or what General C. Robert Kehler, United States Strategic Command (USSTRATCOM) Commander called "hedging."[59] According to Gen Kehler, the current JOPP and JOPE does not account for incorrect assumptions or misinterpretation of the strategic environment. For instance, MCPP ends the planning cycle with a transition brief to the commander.[60] In the final briefing to the commander, branch plans are listed to the commander but not at a level that is even remotely executable or flexible to account for dynamic situation updates and changes. By identifying branch plans that are not fully developed during the MCPP, planners now generate additional operational planning teams (OPT) and essentially isolate the existing plan from the branch plan. If the OPT highlighted contingencies and then planned for them accordingly, it would in turn build a further developed, more realistic plan that accurately portrays events in the battlespace.

Along with needing fully developed contingency plans, OPTs should account for and build contracts between domains to enhance lethality and operations in the battlespace. By accurately addressing the critical role that each asset plays throughout the phases of the operation, a more comprehensive plan is developed.

CONCLUSION

The core of XDS is the ability to leverage capabilities from different domains to "create unique—and often decisive—effects."[61] As United States Joint Force experience in cyberspace continues to evolve, soldiers, sailors, marines, and airmen will continue to determine new ways to solve problems in order to meet strategic national objectives. Figure 1.2 below portrays the cyber relationship among other operational domains. This is crucial to consider because in 21st century warfare, "all domains are interconnected via cyberspace operations."[62]

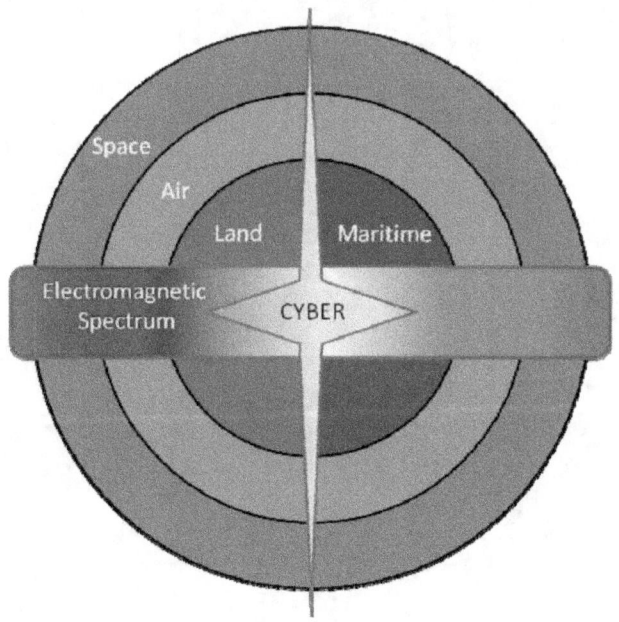

Emerging warfighting domains such as cyberspace and the precipitously changing and dynamic character of globalization have shifted the nature of future warfare. The fabric of American security strategies currently hangs in the balance. Revisions and reviews of how the government of the United States could more effectively protect the national populace have resulted in revisions in documents such as the NSS, NMS, and DSG, shaping the future of the United States Military. Nevertheless, a decade of war and declining economic vitality has hampered the United States Military's ability to fulfill its core competencies. The United States Air Force is leading the charge in developing and refining XDS operations against a near-peer adversary. However, fiscal limitations, unsustainable operations tempos, inadequate training, and current operational planning paradigms and processes have put the United States Military in a perilous situation and hindered its ability to conduct effective and efficient defense. The greatest calamity that could arise from these realities is the inability to address XDS in full-spectrum combat operations against a near-peer adversary.

Endnotes

[1]*The National Military Strategy of the United States of America.* Department of Defense. 2011. Pg 3.

[2]*Joint Operating Access Concept.* Joint Chiefs of Staff. January 17, 2012. Pg. ii.

[3]*Defense Strategic Guidance.* Department of Defense. January 2012. Pg. 5.

[4]*The Implications of Military Spending Cuts for NATOs Largest Members.* Center on the United States and Europe at Brookings. July 2012. Pg. 26.

[5]Michael Donley and Mark Welsh. *Fiscal Year 2013 (FY13) Near Term Actions to Mitigate Sequestration.* Memorandum for the Deputy Secretary of Defense. January 7, 2013. Pg. 1.

[6]*Defense Budget Priorities and Choices.* Department of Defense. January 2012. Pg 1.

[5]*The National Security Strategy.* The White House. May 2012. Pg 14.

[8]Joseph Blady, M.D., *What Sequestration Means for the Department of Defense.* The Huffington Post. August 21, 2012. http://www.huffingtonpost.com/joseph-blady-md/sequestration-department-of-defense_b_1819341.html.

[9]NMS. Pg. 9.

[10]Tim Arango and Michael Schmidt. *Last Convoy of American Troops Leave Iraq.* New York Times. December 18, 2011. http://www.nytimes.com/2011/12/19/world/middleeast/last-convoy-of-american-troops-leaves-iraq.html?pagewanted=all&_moc.semityn.www.

[11]Smith, King, De Jesus, Pilve, and Nelson. *The Impact of Frequent Deployments on Military Readiness.* United States Army Sergeants Major Academy. 2007. Pg. 2.

[12]NMS. Pg. 18.

[13]C. Castro and A. Adler. *Operations tempo (OPTEMPO): Preface to the special issue.* Military Psychology. 2005. Pg. 131.

[14]J. Hosek, J. Kavanagh, and L. Miller. *How deployments affect service members.* Santa Monica, CA: Rand Corporation. 2006. Pg. 2.

[15]Donald H. Rumsfeld. *Annual report to the president and the congress.* 2005. Pg. 2.

[16]*Quadrennial Defense Review Report.* Office of the Secretary of Defense. 2006. Pg. 6.

[17]*Status of Forces Survey of Active Duty Members.* Defense Manpower Data Center. 2008. Pg. 109.

[18]*Status of Forces Survey of Active Duty Members.* Pg. 130.

[19]*Status of Forces Survey of Active Duty Members.* Pg. 166.

[20]Castro & Adler. Pg. 133.

[21]Smith, King, De Jesus, Pilve, and Nelson. Pg. 2.

[22]NMS. Pg. 2.

[23]Smith, King, De Jesus, Pilve, and Nelson. Pg. 2.

[24]*Office of the Secretary of Defense, Ground Force Equipment Repair, Replacement, and Recapitalization Requirements Resulting from Sustained Combat Operations.* Office of the Secretary of Defense. April 2005. p. 2.

[25]Smith, King, De Jesus, Pilve, and Nelson. Pg. 11.

[26]Smith, King, De Jesus, Pilve, and Nelson. Pg.11.

[27]Smith, King, De Jesus, Pilve, and Nelson. Pg. 11.

[28]Smith, King, De Jesus, Pilve, and Nelson. Pg. 11.

[29]NSS. Pg 14.

[30]NMS. Pg. 20.

[31]Tod R. Fingal (Commander 414 CTS), interview by Major John Gallemore, April 2, 2013.

[32]Air Force Instruction 11-2F16-V1, RAP Tasking Message. *F-16CM Blk 50/52 Ready Aircrew Program (RAP) Tasking Memorandum, AS-12 Change 1.* April 1, 2012. Pg. 10.

[33]Air Force Instruction 11-2F16-V1. Pg. 10.

[34]Air Force Instruction 11-2F16-V1. Pg. 10.

[35]*F-16 Fighting Falcon.* Global Security.org. Retrieved September 19, 2012. http://www.globalsecurity.org/military/systems/aircraft/f-16-life.htm. Pg. 2.

[36]NSS. Pg. 18.

[37]*RED FLAG-NELLIS Exercise 12-3 Final Report.* 414 Combat Training Squadron. Nellis AFB. Air Combat Command. March 2012. Pg. 1.

[38]*RED FLAG-NELLIS Exercise 12-3 Final Report.* Pg. 2.

[39]JCS Pub 3-30. *Command and Control for Joint Air Operations.* January 12, 2010. Pg.

II-2.

[40] JCS Pub 3-60. *Joint Targeting.* April 13, 2007. Pg. ix.

[41] *RED FLAG-NELLIS Exercise 12-3 Final Report.* Pg. 4.

[42] *RED FLAG-NELLIS Exercise 12-3 Final Report.* Pg. 8.

[43] *RED FLAG-NELLIS Exercise 12-3 Final Report.* Pg. 15.

[44] *RED FLAG-NELLIS Exercise 12-3 Final Report.* Pg. 19.

[45] Fingal. April 2, 2013.

[46] Fingal. April 2, 2013.

[47] *Capstone Concept for Joint Operations: Joint Force 2020.* Chairman of the Joint Chiefs of Staff. September 10, 2012. Pg. 8.

[48] *RED FLAG-NELLIS Exercise 12-3 Final Report.* Pg. 15.

[49] CCJO. Pg. 12.

[50] CJCSI 3500.01G. *Joint Training Policy and Guidance for the Armed Forces of the United States.* CJCS. March 15, 2012. Figure 1.

[51] CJCSI. Pg. A-4.

[52] CJCS Pub 3-0. *Joint Operations.* Chairman of the Joint Chiefs of Staff. Aug 11, 2011. Pg. I-8.

[53] CJCS Pub 3-0. Pg. II-1.

[54] CJCS Pub 3-0. Pg. II-2.

[55] Carl von Clausewitz, *On War,* ed. Michael Howard and Peter Paret. Princeton, NJ: Princeton University Press, 1984. Pg. 143.

[56] Planner's Handbook for Operational Design. *Joint Staff, J-7 Joint and Coalition Warfighting..* Oct 7, 2011. Pg. I-2.

[57] CJCS Pub 3-0. Pg. I-11.

[58] Maj Raymond Daniel. *ME3-(PC)2: A Problem Solving Methodology.* United States Air Force Weapons School. June 29, 2009. Pg. 14.

[59] General C. Robert Kehler. "Perspectives from Commander, USSTRATCOM." (lecture, Marine Corps University, Quantico, VA, January 16, 2013).

[60] MWCP 5-1. *Marine Corps Planning Process*. U.S. Marine Corps. Aug 24, 2010. Pg. 7-2.

[61] AFDD 3-12. *Cyberspace Operations.* U.S. Air Force. November 30, 2011. Pg. 19.

[62] AFDD 3-12. Pg. 19.

Bibliography

AFDD 3-12. *Cyberspace Operations.* U.S. Air Force. November 30, 2011.

Air Force Instruction 11-2F16-V1, RAP Tasking Message. *F-16CM Blk 50/52 Ready Aircrew Program (RAP) Tasking Memorandum, AS-12 Change 1.* April 1, 2012.

Arango, Tim and Schmidt, Michael. *Last Convoy of American Troops Leave Iraq.* New York Times. December 18, 2011. http://www.nytimes.com/2011/12/19/world/middleeast/last-convoy-of-american-troops-leaves-iraq.html?pagewanted=all&_moc.semityn.www.

Blady, Joseph, M.D., *What Sequestration Means for the Department of Defense.* The Huffington Post. August 21, 2012. http://www.huffingtonpost.com/joseph-blady-md/sequestration-department-of-defense_b_1819341.html.

Capstone Concept for Joint Operations: Joint Force 2020. Chairman of the Joint Chiefs of Staff. September 10, 2012.

Castro, C. and Adler, A., *Operations tempo (OPTEMPO): Preface to the special issue.* Military Psychology. 2005.

CJCS Pub 3-0. *Joint Operations.* Chairman of the Joint Chiefs of Staff. Aug 11, 2011.

CJCSI 3500.01G. *Joint Training Policy and Guidance for the Armed Forces of the United States.* CJCS. March 15, 2012.

Clausewitz, Carl von. *On War,* Edited, Michael Howard and Peter Paret. Princeton, NJ: Princeton University Press, 1984.

Daniel, Raymond, Maj. *ME3-(PC)2: A Problem Solving Methodology.* United States Air Force Weapons School. June 29, 2009.

Defense Budget Priorities and Choices. Department of Defense. January 2012.

Defense Strategic Guidance. Department of Defense. January 2012.

Donley, Michael and Welsh, Mark. *Fiscal Year 2013 (FY13) Near Term Actions to Mitigate Sequestration.* Memorandum for the Deputy Secretary of Defense. January 7, 2013.

F-16 Fighting Falcon. Global Security.org. Retrieved September 19, 2012. http://www.globalsecurity.org/military/systems/aircraft/f-16-life.htm.

FM 5-0. *The Operations Process.* U.S. Army. March, 2010.

Hosek, Kavanagh, Miller. *How deployments affect service members.* Santa Monica, CA: Rand Corporation. 2006.

JCS Pub 3-30. *Command and Control for Joint Air Operations.* January 12, 2010.

JCS Pub 3-60. *Joint Targeting.* April 13, 2007.

JCS Pub 5-0. *Joint Operations Planning.* Chairman of the Joint Chiefs of Staff. Aug 11, 2011.

Joint Operating Access Concept. Joint Chiefs of Staff. January 17, 2012.

Joint Operating Environment. United States Joint Forces Command. February 18, 2010.

Kehler, General C. Robert. "Perspectives from Commander, USSTRATCOM." Strategic Communication Lecture Series, Marine Corps University, Quantico, VA, January 16, 2013.

Kugler, Richard. *New Directions in National Security Strategy, Defense Plans, and Diplomacy.* Center for National and Security Policy. NDU Press. 2011.

MWCP 5-1. *Marine Corps Planning Process.* U.S. Marine Corps. Aug 24, 2010.

Office of the Secretary of Defense, Ground Force Equipment Repair, Replacement, and Recapitalization Requirements Resulting from Sustained Combat Operations. Office of the Secretary of Defense. April 2005.

Planner's Handbook for Operational Design. Joint Staff, J-7 Joint and Coalition Warfighting. Oct 7, 2011.

Quadrennial Defense Review Report. Office of the Secretary of Defense. 2006.

RED FLAG-NELLIS Exercise 12-3 Final Report. 414 Combat Training Squadron. Nellis AFB. Air Combat Command. March 2012.

Rumsfield, Donald H., *Annual report to the president and the congress.* 2005.

Schwartz, Norman and Greenert, Jonathan. *Air-Sea Battle.* The American Interest. February 20, 2012.

Smith, King, De Jesus, Pilve, and Nelson. *The Impact of Frequent Deployments on Military Readiness.* United States Army Sergeants Major Academy. 2007.

Status of Forces Survey of Active Duty Members. Defense Manpower Data Center. 2008.

The Implications of Military Spending Cuts for NATOs Largest Members. Center on the United States and Europe at Brookings. July 2012.

The National Defense Strategy. The White House. 2011.

The National Military Strategy of the United States of America. Department of Defense. 2011.

The National Security Strategy. The White House. May 2012.

www.ingramcontent.com/pod-product-compliance
Lightning Source LLC
Chambersburg PA
CBHW080743290526
45790CB00008B/3305